Spiritua

Spiritual Warfare
A Handbook

SANDRA RONE MIRELES

Spiritual Warfare A Handbook

Copyright © 2008 by Sandra Rone Mireles. All rights reserved. No portion of this book may be reproduced, stored in a retrieval system, or transmitted in any form or by any means—electronic, mechanical, photo copy, recording, or any other—except for brief quotations in printed reviews, without the prior permission of the publisher. Cover design and art copyright©2008 Mark Mireles.

Spiritual Warfare A Handbook

Awesome God, Awesome Friend

Lord, You are my friend. I talk to you all the time. You make me feel *so* close to you, Sometimes I forget that you are also That wonderful majestic Creator of the universe. At times I address you so casually that it might seem disrespectful...*How could I so easily take You For granted?* When I first met you the awesome Holiness of your Presence Over-whelmed me! The love, comfort and friendship You offered *pierced my soul!* I have never been the same. Failure has been a part of my life *so* often, and yet *you have never* Failed me. There have been times of sorrow that left my heart an open wound. It was then that you wrapped your Arms around me with unconditional Love. I felt your heart beat with mine! You felt my pain. You were there. The crowning joy of my life has been your love for me. You are an Awesome God and an Awesome Friend.

© Copyright by Sandra Mireles TGBTG
22 March 2001
Inspired by the memory of
Imogene Kilgore

Spiritual Warfare A Handbook

Dedication

To my father in the Lord, Reverend Clark E. Lott, Sr., PhD. who taught me the word of God when I was a child. It was the best gift in the world and has stood the test of time. I thank you.

To Reverend James L. Kilgore and Imogene Kilgore who loved us, and welcomed us into their hearts when we were in desperate need of a spiritual home. I thank you.

To my pastor Reverend Myrick Johnson, who is a strong leader and who gave us a spiritual home. I thank you.

Spiritual Warfare A Handbook

Acknowledgement

This book is dedicated to my family and friends who know of my many encounters with my adversary, who understand the power of my adversary, and helped me pray through them.

My husband Sam Mireles

My mother Janette Rone

Glenda Marshall

Cindy Mitchell

Mark Mireles

Derek Mireles

Spiritual Warfare A Handbook

Preface

My purpose in writing Spiritual Warfare A Handbook, is to *inform* and offer help to those who need to know that they are not crazy. They do not suffer from an over active imagination, and they are not alone. This book is not for everyone. I am acutely aware that some of you will look on this book as the work of a fanatic or a fool. You may think it the work of a person with a large imagination and completely beyond the realm of possibility.

However, those of you who suffer spiritual attacks will immediately feel a kinship with my story. My message for you is to pray on. Take authority over your adversary. Know that God is with you and understands your need. I do not know why some Christians are tormented by the adversary and some never feel his presence. This question has troubled me for many years.

I strongly believe that it is impossible to measure a person's spirituality by whether or not he or she is plagued by spiritual attacks. I believe a person who is attacked is forced to grow stronger or suffer torment. But I do not believe that a person can boast they are more spiritual because of their ability to overcome the attacks of the devil. Jesus warned us to rejoice that our names are written in the Book of Life and not to rejoice that the demons are subject to us. This book is meant to be a study guide and a handbook useful for Bible Study to which you can refer again and again. May God richly bless you and may you enjoy your journey!

Sandra Rone Mireles

Spiritual Warfare A Handbook

FROM A LAYMAN'S POINT OF VIEW
SPIRITUAL WARFARE: A HANDBOOK!

- Introduction
- Birthright
- Understanding the Battle
- Acknowledging Spiritual Encounters
- Prayer, Prayer, and more Prayer
    - Do You Pray
    - Worship
    - Learning How to Approach the Throne
    - Meditation
    - Pray Without Ceasing
    - Enjoying Conversation With the Lord
- Are you ready for a fight?
- Getting Ready for the Fight
- Dealing With Fear
- Inner Conflict
- Absolute Trust
- Winning the war
- What are these Spiritual Weapons?
- Examples of Spiritual Encounters
- Last Word

Introduction

What do you think about the devil? Is he a boogie man to frighten children? Is he a myth? Do you believe the devil is a living sentient being? He has been called by many names. His name was Lucifer when he was the *star of the morning* and led the angels in worship of God Almighty! He was beautiful, proud, arrogant, and haughty. He was a deceiver who convinced one third of the angels *(Revelations 12:4)* to turn against their Creator and make war in the heavens. He has been called many names since ancient times; including Satan, Asmodai, Beelzebub, and Lucifer.

What is the devil? In simple terms the devil is a fallen angel, pure evil, who lead one-third of the angelic host to war against God. He and the other fallen angels were cast from heaven by the Archangel Michael and the heavenly Host during the time before the earth was formed and man was created. He is the accuser of the brethren *(Revelations 12:10)*, and has endless patience. His mission is to bring accusation and torment into your life while keeping you at odds with God. Satan's influence is responsible for most of the broken hearts, marriages, minds, and lives since the creation of man. While Satan does not have the power to take the life of a spirit-filled child of God, his influence is strong and it is important to have the tools necessary to keep him in his place.

One morning long ago Satan came dancing into the heavenlies with the angelic host for morning worship. God challenged him to take the measure of his servant Job. Satan agreed that Job loved God, but made this ringing accusation, "Take away the hedge you have set about him and then see if he will not curse you". (Paraphrased) When God agreed to allow the devil to test Job in everything but in taking his life, there followed one of the great trials of human experience. Job lost his wealth, his children, and suffered greatly in his body. His friends turned against him and even his wife advised him to, "Curse God and die". When pushed beyond human endurance, Job dared to question God; The Lord turned on him with such a lecture it took four full chapters to get it all down (Job 38-42). It is well worth reading as an example of what to expect if you decide to contend with the Almighty. And yet when all was said and done, God loved Job and rewarded him by giving him wealth; restoring to him more children and the respect of his friends. Many religious theologians believe that the story of Job is a myth. I choose to believe that Job lived, and his experience was an example of what we may expect in our encounters with Satan in our daily lives.

We must understand Satan's position in the universe. The devil is *not* equal to God. He is not omniscient (all knowing) and certainly does not know what you are thinking. He is *not* a mind reader. He can *not* be in all places at all times. It is highly unlikely that many (if any) of us have actually encountered the devil *himself* at any time in our lives. The devil has many fallen angels who have permanent assignments in the world and carry out their assigned duties with vigor! These fallen angels are formed into groups where they rule according to their talents. Think about how you feel about the city or town where you live. Is there an area that is known for certain crimes? Do you know of areas where theft is common, rape or murder? Many of these fallen angels are nothing more than *familiar spirits* whose purpose it is to spy on people and report their findings to more powerful demons that carry out the mission; *whatever that may be*. These demons are characterized by their names such as anger, hatred, lust, bitterness, lying, stealing, adultery, homosexuality, murder...the list goes on and on. When one is targeted by the full force of such demon activity it can be hard to resist. A person without the spirit of the Lord within can be at the mercy of such evil beings. Even spirit filled Christians find themselves at a loss as to how to deal with such bitter attacks. Know this, *any* and *every* time you decide to challenge the activities of the devil when his demons are attacking your life or the life of your loved one, there *will be* a price to pay if you win against him. Satan is a sore loser and he will use everything in his arsenal against you to bring you down. He fights dirty and nothing will be left out or forgotten. It is a fight to the death.

We are living in the perilous times spoken of by Timothy (*II Timothy 3: 1-9).* Wickedness is a way of life, and the television has made us comfortable with sin as it is dished up to us night after night in our living rooms. Nudity, sexual immorality, and every sort of perversion are freely available to anyone; including our children who have access to television or the internet via their personal computer. This discussion is not about whether or not it is a sin to bring a television into the home. A television, radio, computer, CD player, ipod, mp3 player, or any other entertainment medium is nothing more than a tool to be used at the discretion of the individual who owns it. Satan uses these tools for entertainment as a means to destroy the moral values of society as a whole. It is the responsibility of every spirit filled Christian to monitor the entertainment brought into the home and block inappropriate music, movies, and television programs. These are not the only tools the devil uses against us. This is merely the short list in a very long arsenal of weapons Satan uses against humanity.

The apostle Peter gave us a hint of things to come as well as our responsibility in dealing with this threat in *II Peter 5:8-9 "Be sober, be vigilant; because your adversary the devil, as a roaring lion, walketh about, seeking whom he may devour: (9) Whom resist steadfast in the faith, knowing that the same afflictions are accomplished in your brethren that are in the world (KJV).*

We are clearly warned that we will have encounters with the devil. Difficult times require us to gain an understanding of exactly what we are up against so that we may overcome. God has created a plan for the spirit-filled believer to overcome the devices of the devil. The purpose of this book is to offer a handbook of information to be used against the tricks of the devil whenever he or his fallen angels come against you.

This discussion began with a very important question. *What do you think about the devil?* Your answer to this question will guide your path to enlightenment. For those of you who have never encountered the devil, or did not recognize the encounter for what it was; it is possible that you will feel this book is a work of fantasy or the work of a misguided fanatic. However, for those readers who *have* encountered Satan and been tormented by his oppression; this book is for you. Jesus told us plainly in John 8:32 *"And ye shall know the truth, and the truth shall make you free."*

There is no doubt that Jesus Christ conquered sin, death, hell, and the grave when he gave His life on the cross at Calvary. Satan lost his battle for control on that day. And yet...he fights on! He refuses to give ground in his war against the Saints and will never stop fighting until the final moment when Jesus returns to catch away his Bride and beyond. It is my intention to offer practical suggestions that will dispel the misunderstanding about our *rights* as Children of God, as well as tools to help in dealing with the adversary.

Prayer

Father, help me to understand that the devil is a fierce enemy of the saints. Please show me how to take authority over my adversary through the power of the Holy Spirit that you bestowed upon me. In Jesus Name.

Birthright

You have a birthright inheritance. Every person who has been born again according to the Biblical instruction has a birthright. This birthright comes immediately upon the indwelling of the Holy Spirit in your heart. In its simplest terms the birthright is an inheritance. Understanding the role of the birthright in the Old Testament is very important because it gives a glimpse of the importance of the spiritual birthright of every born again Christian. In ancient Israel the first born child received the father's blessing and a double portion of the family estate. This generally included land and cattle, sheep, goats, etc. The birthright was divided among the children by dividing the number of children plus one into the total portion of the inheritance. The eldest son received two portions. This was a great honor and was not to be despised. Abraham's grandsons, Jacob and Esau were twins. Jacob came out of the womb holding onto the heel of his brother Esau. As the elder the birthright *belonged* to Esau. And yet Esau did not treasure this great gift and sold it to his brother for a pot of stew *(Genesis 25:29)*. Unlike Esau, Jacob knew the value of the birthright and plotted to get it.

Genesis 25:29 and Jacob sod pottage; and Esau came in from the field and he was faint. (30) And Esau said to Jacob: 'Let me swallow, I pray thee, some of this red, red pottage; for I am faint.' Therefore was his name called Edom. (31) And Jacob said: 'Sell me first thy birthright.' (32) And Esau said: 'Behold, I am at the point to die; and what profit shall the birthright do to me?'(33) And Jacob said: 'Swear to me first'; and he swore unto him; and he sold his birthright unto Jacob. (34) And Jacob gave Esau bread and pottage of lentils; and he did eat and drink, and rose up, and went his way. So Esau despised his birthright.

The passing of the birthright into the family of Jacob and his heirs changed the course of history. Eventually the line of the Kings of Israel was born to this family. Jesus Christ was born to the tribe of Judah. Esau's lack of foresight and respect for his heritage sent him and his heirs into obscurity while the descendents of Jacob have never been forgotten.

As children of God we have a birthright. It is part of the inheritance left to us by Jesus Christ and redeemed when we were filled with his Holy Spirit. This birthright offers great power and confidence in God for those who understand what it is and what it means to each of us. So *what is* the birthright of the children of God? This is your gift when you receive the Holy Ghost. This list is not in the scriptural order. It is not complete. See below.

1. Power
2. Tongues (heavenly language)
3. Ability to witness
4. Cast out demons
5. They will lay hands on the sick who will be healed
6. They will take up serpents (if they are bitten by a snake accidentally it will not hurt them)

7. If they drink (or eat) anything deadly it will not hurt them
8. One who believes on Jesus Christ and the works that he did will do greater works than those done by Jesus Christ because Jesus rose up to be with the Father.
9. Anything you ask in the name of Jesus Christ will be done to reveal the glory of the Father in the Son. Anything the believer asks in the name of Jesus Christ will be done.

Every item in the preceding list is mentioned in the following Bible verses. These privileges are plainly and explicitly stated. There are no qualifiers. These privileges are stated as a fact. That means that **all believers** who follow Jesus Christ and are filled with the spirit **will (be able to)** demonstrate these signs and activities in their lives. This handbook talks about birthright gift number 4, "they will cast out demons".

17 "And these signs will follow those who believe: In My name they will cast out demons; they will speak with new tongues;
18 "they will take up serpents; and if they drink

anything deadly, it will by no means hurt them; they will lay hands on the sick, and they will recover." Mark 16:17-20

*But ye shall **receive power**, after that the Holy Ghost is come upon you: and ye shall be witnesses unto me both in Jerusalem, and in all Judaea, and in Samaria, and unto the uttermost part of the earth. Acts 1:8*

"Verily, verily, I say unto you, He that believeth on me, the works that I do shall he do also; and greater works than these shall he do; because I go unto my Father. And whatsoever ye shall ask in my name that will I do, that the Father may be glorified in the Son. If ye shall ask any thing in my name, I will do it" John 14:12-14.

It is important to understand the message Jesus sent to us during the days of His teaching on earth. The disciples and early Christian believers understood exactly how much power they had received upon the infilling of the Holy Spirit. Today many of us simply do not get it. We do not have a good understanding of exactly what God has given us by dwelling within our hearts and bodies. It is important for the believer to gain an understanding of the awesome gift of God that we have. We not only have access to miracles, signs, and wonders; it is *expected* that we live in such a manner that these demonstrated signs of faith are evident in our daily lives. This means for the purpose of this discussion that we do not have to tolerate interference from the devil or the fallen angels (demons) in our homes or in the lives of our families.

Of course, these are strong words and it is easy to say that it is intolerable for the devil to torment and influence us as Christians. We have heard it preached that Satan was defeated when Jesus died on the cross and rose again the third day! We know this is true but we have difficulty understanding how to put into practice our fight against this strong enemy. How do we successfully deal with the reality of demon oppression and interference in our lives? We become distressed, and defeated when we are not successful at keeping the devil from destroying our families! There is a way out! The first thing you need know is that defeat is **not** an option. The **power** of the **Holy Spirit** that is resident in each spirit-filled believer makes defeat a no-brainer! We *cannot* accept defeat!

Points to Ponder:
Read over the list of Birthright gifts available to the believer when he/she is filled with the Holy Spirit. Meditate on each one and accept that these ...*traits,* for lack of a better word are meant to be active in the life of every believer.

Search your heart and ask yourself these questions:

1. Do I *really* believe that I have Birthright gifts from the Lord? (Well, do I?)

2. What do I really think about the devil? Is he real? Is he a myth? What do I *really* believe? (This is a very important point to ponder. You must know where you stand.)

3. Does the devil really attack people or is that something made up by the fanciful or fanatics? (What do I believe?)

4. If I do believe in the Birthright, what does that mean for me?

Spend time in prayer seeking God to help you decide what you believe. Jot down scriptures that you find are helpful in your battle with your enemy.

Prayer

Heavenly Father please give me a clear understanding of the Birthright gifts you gave me when I was filled with your spirit. Teach me to appreciate the great sacrifice you made for my sins through the death of your son Jesus Christ. I want to know you in spirit and in truth.

Notes

_____
_____
_____
_____
_____
_____
_____
_____
_____
_____
_____
_____
_____
_____

Understanding the Battle

We are in a fight for our very lives and for our souls! Make no mistake about it. The battle goes on every moment of every day. There may be times when we pull back from the fight because we need to rest...or hide in the shadow of the Rock, but eventually we rejoin the war because it is the only way to achieve victory in our lives and in the lives of those around us.

For we do not wrestle against flesh and blood, but against principalities, against powers, against the rulers of the darkness of this age, against spiritual hosts of wickedness in the heavenly places... Ephesians 6: 12

Paul, in his letter to the Ephesians made it clear what we are up against. It is important for Twenty-first century believers to know that the devil is *alive and well* and his mission has not changed. If anything, he is even more determined because he knows that his time is limited.

Know this...the closer you walk with the Lord, the more determined your adversary will be to hinder your progress! He will come at you through the behavior of your spouse, your children, in-laws, co-workers, or other people with whom you come into regular contact. He may use your brothers and sisters in the Lord to do his evil deeds. If you are weak, he will whisper in your ears angry thoughts, tempting thoughts, etc. There may be times when Satan fills your mind with images of worthlessness, laziness, anger, feelings that your pastor does not like you, the church fellowship is against you, and many *many* other thoughts. The devil cannot force anyone to do anything. However, he may torment you in your dreams...he may give you nightmares, or brazenly appear in your dreams to challenge your beliefs. He may appear literally in your presence. He is a liar and a deceiver, and may attempt to woo you with promises. Satan has been around a long time and he is wise in the ways of the world. He studies the scripture and knows exactly how to twist the Holy Words to suit his purpose. This is proven in Genesis when the serpent tempted Eve to eat from the forbidden tree of knowledge. He twisted the scripture to his own purpose deceiving Eve who was not as knowledgeable.

Satan may influence your companions to say horrible angry things to you. Anyone may be susceptible to the whisperings of the demons at any time. It is important to be aware of your thoughts and how you react to ideas that come into your mind. He may come at you with oppression (A feeling of being heavily weighed down in mind or body). He may cause you to become depressed when there is no reason for this to happen. I am personally acquainted with a man who *suddenly* found himself with self esteem issues and a feeling of total worthlessness. This feeling endured for almost a month until he sought help from another believer. When it was pointed out to him that he had never felt like this before in his life and this feeling was something that had suddenly appeared in his mind, he joined together in prayer with another believer and together in the Power of the Holy Ghost in the Name of Jesus Christ, this spirit of oppression was banished and left immediately. He had never before or since felt such feelings. He was *delivered instantly!*

Satan may attack you physically as he did Job. He may bring real or imagined sickness or pain into your life. It is important to understand when these illnesses appear that they are manifestations of something bigger happening in your life. Now, I am not saying that every time you get a cold Satan has attacked you physically. You must be the judge of whether you are really sick or whether you have something wrong that comes from another source. Remember that Satan is a liar. He is a very good liar, and his workers have had an eternity of experience to develop their skills. In my experience one does not manifest many different illnesses in your body during the same time period and find that the illness is real. For example, I suddenly experienced pain in my right knee that was excruciating. I knew there was no reason for this pain. God had just healed me of Arthritis so I knew the pain could not be real. I rebuked the pain in the Name of Jesus and it went away. The next day I experienced pain in the left knee. Again I rebuked the pain and it disappeared. During the same week I experienced agonizing pain in my left hand where God had healed my arthritis. On that day I was suddenly convinced that my hand would be crippled and would never be well. When I realized the direction my thoughts were taking I again rebuked the thoughts and the pain in the Name of Jesus and the thoughts and pain left me. When these types of attacks come in different areas of your mind or body during a short period of time it is easy to recognize that this is not normal body function. I have been attacked in my respiratory system, bones, general pain, as well as mental or emotional pain. I have been attacked by a period of unexpected anger and rage. When I recognized that this anger was not normal I went to the church and prayed until God bound the spirit and removed it from my life.

When these attacks come it is imperative for you to search your heart and take action. You must first analyze your situation and decide if this is a demonic attack or if this is something you brought on yourself. It is important to understand that the devil is not responsible for every problem we face in life. For instance, if you spend too much money and run short before pay day, it is *not* an attack of the devil. If you are ticketed for speeding in your car, *you must not* blame the devil for putting the police officer in the right place to catch you! You must obey the law! Satan has nothing to do with these incidents. If *your* behavior brings something bad into your life, do not blame the devil for making this happen! You are a free will agent and make your own choices. *You* are *accountable* for the choices you make. The devil is happy to watch you suffer, but he *cannot* take the credit for the happening.

While it is true that Satan can influence you, your spouse, or both of you; causing a fight, you must think about what happened to understand whether this is really something supernatural. It is possible that you just simply had a fight. I have heard of couples who never said a cross word to each other, but that is not the norm. Everybody disagrees eventually. My purpose in offering these examples is to make it clear that Satan and his fallen angels interact with us daily. But, we *cannot* blame the devil every time we have a disagreement, a problem, or accident. There *will be* times when there is *no other possible reason* why things happen. *This is the time* we must be able to deal with the crisis presented by the evil forces that surround us.

> 31And the Lord said, Simon, Simon, behold,
> Satan hath desired to have you, that he may sift
> you as wheat: 32But I have prayed for thee,

that thy faith fail not: and when thou art converted, strengthen thy brethren. Luke 22

Jesus was talking with his disciples in the book of Luke. He told Simon, "Satan wants to sift you as wheat". This means that Satan wanted to torment Simon terribly. When wheat is sifted it is shaken to separate the parts of the wheat from the chaff. When Satan comes against us he will shake us to the very foundation of our being. His goal is to make us doubt our beliefs, our experience, and *even* our walk with God. Jesus stated two things in verse 32:

1. He prayed for Simon that his faith would not fail...
2. And that when he was converted; he would strengthen his brethren

This is a very clear statement that Jesus was not merely telling Simon that Satan was only interested in tormenting him. Jesus wanted him to know that they were *all* to be victimized by Satan, but it would be in their power through faith to be over comers. These statements make it clear that we will be sorely tried by the devil and that it will take *all our strength* to keep the faith as well as help our fellow believers overcome the snares of the devil that may block their path.

It is *imperative* that we understand the battle that lies before us when we decide to engage our adversary. It is one thing to know that Satan is focusing his attacks on your family or in other personal areas of your life. It is quite another thing to feel confident or ready to engage the forces of the enemy in a head-on frontal spiritual attack. Spiritual Warfare is emotionally draining and physically exhausting. It is not to be undertaken by the fearful or faint of heart! It takes a strong person to recognize when the adversary is or has been interfering in his or her life, and be *willing* to put a stop to it! There will be times when you will not be up to the challenge and you know it. At these times you will retreat into the shelter of the protection of the Lord who will guard your mind and body from the snares of the devil. You will stay close to God, and keep His Word close to your heart with his comforting arms around you all the time. There is nothing wrong with retreating to a place of safety in God. There is an old song that has been sung in my church for as long as I can remember. It goes like this:

He's my comfort when I'm weary,

He's my shelter from the storm...

He's my armor...when in battle

And in the cold....He keeps me warm!

(Author unknown)

God *can* be everything to you. It is up to you to decide how much of God you want to experience in your life. The words of this song express exactly how God desires to interact with His children. The onus is on *you* to decide exactly how much you are willing to allow God to manifest His Spirit in your life. Your adversary will attack you. He will make you afraid, worried, tearful, sad, and miserable if he can accomplish it. He will oppress the minds of your family members, or possibly even you, the reader. It is up to you to recognize the negative thoughts that appear in your mind at inappropriate moments for what they are... demonic whisperings to cloud your judgment. There may be times in your life when you see that Satan has attacked someone close to you and you feel helpless to do anything about it.

You may feel helpless because (1) you know you are not up to the fight (2) you do not know how to fight (3) you have just come out of a spiritual battle and have a very good understanding of what you are up against. The truth about battling the devil is that until you have done it you cannot gain a true understanding of what Spiritual Warfare is all about. I am using the term battling the devil very particularly. Most of us have felt that we are beset by evil at times in our lives. My meaning when I say *battling the devil* refers to actively working against the devil in a spirit of travail through intercessory prayer. This type of prayer is exhausting and difficult. However, if you ever come to see how horribly Satan has interfered in your life you will want to do everything in your power to stop him at all costs!

We are living in difficult times. The society we live in makes excuses for the sins of people while condemning believers who try to live a holy life. Haters of God are working to remove the Ten Commandments from every government building in America while removing the words 'In God We Trust' from our money. These people never give up; they say that we are free to practice our religious beliefs in private but that there is no room in the public sector for religious expression. At the same time this is happening, world religion and the worship of false, man made gods is becoming more prevalent in America. These religions bring the spirits of their demon gods into our lives.

Never has there been a time in American history when Christianity is so misrepresented, and the beliefs of our forefathers skewed with lies and innuendo that confuses the average person. The time has come for spirit-filled believers to arm themselves with the Truth; and the Knowledge of how to deal with these demonic attacks.

Points to Ponder:

- You *must understand the battle* before you can join the fight. You must accept that Satan with his fallen angels are your enemy and are to be

found everywhere. If you *do not believe this you will never* be able to join the battle against their control.
- You must understand that when you challenge the devil *there will be a price to pay*. You cannot hope to win if you do not maintain *an active prayer life*. You must know that your adversary will not give up easily. When you overcome one battle, he comes back with another one from another angle.
- You must take your birthright seriously and *know* that *you have* the right to challenge your adversary when he comes against you and your family. This is the first step in your spiritual growth.
- You must understand that while it is certainly one of the signs of the believers that you will be able to cast out demons; the novice should never attempt to do such a thing. You are much like a baby who drinks milk until his body matures and is able to tolerate meat. Learn everything you can about living the life before getting involved in spiritual warfare.

- Remember to *never* rejoice because the demons are subject to you. Celebrate that your name is written in heaven.
- Understand that with privilege comes responsibility. God gives us the birth right gifts when we receive His Spirit into our lives. These gifts were not given so that we might rest on our good deeds and pat ourselves on the back in a spirit of superiority. God expects us to accept the gifts He has given us with humility. When we understand what we have received, we are to use the gifts to bless others who come into our lives. We do not exist in a vacuum. Hurting people who need what we have to offer are all around us. Think about it.

17And the seventy returned again with joy, saying, Lord, even the devils are subject unto us through thy name.

18And he said unto them, I beheld Satan as lightning fall from heaven.

19Behold, I give unto you power to tread on serpents and scorpions, and over all the power of the enemy: and nothing shall by any means hurt you.

20Notwithstanding in this rejoice not, that the spirits are subject unto you; but rather rejoice, because your names are written in heaven. Luke 10:17-20 (King James Version)

Prayer

Father, I thank you for giving me power over my adversary. Please help me to remain humble and never forget that my power comes from you. My strength comes from you and is not my own. I give you praise and glory. In Jesus Name.

Acknowledging Spiritual Encounters

One of the hardest things a person will do is admit to others that strange things are happening to them. Fear of being thought crazy, mentally unbalanced, and just totally off your rocker is the reason many people suffer in silence. In some circles discussion of the paranormal is totally accepted, but it is not something that most of the world is willing to acknowledge. Pentecostals are no longer the ignorant, uneducated, gullible people of the past. Most of us no longer live on the wrong side of the tracks and cannot be referred to as Holy Rollers in the real sense. That is not to say that we no longer enjoy a freedom of worship that includes dancing in the spirit and running the aisles. We do.

While this age of enlightenment is a wonderful thing, and we have certainly not changed our doctrinal stance or our freedom of worship; our enlightenment has come at a price. We are aware that talk of the devil is not fashionable and is looked on as something of a myth or fairy tale. Fearing ridicule we keep our experiences to ourselves. We, as a people, still believe that the devil is a real, sentient being and still stalks the human race with evil purposes in mind. But...we do not like to talk about personal encounters with our adversary. Many people believe that speaking about such things bring them closer to you. To some extent I accept this as well because if your adversary has placed a *familiar spirit* with you he will soon know your thoughts and plans. It is important to take into account the gift that lies within you. Learning to live a life that does not give place to the devil takes time. Some thoughts should never be spoken, but one should never hide the need to get help from another child of God. You need a prayer partner!

Selecting your prayer partner is one of the most important things you will ever do in your life. Your prayer partner is **not** someone with whom you gossip about people in the church. This person should not offer negative comments that bring you down. Your prayer partner should be someone who understands your thoughts about spiritual attacks and encounters. This person should be one to whom you feel comfortable talking about anything in your life. You should be able to call your prayer partner for prayer on a moment's notice.

Now, here is a paradox! Satan will attack you and torment you while waking and sleeping. Then he will mock you and say that you are losing your mind because it is not really happening. Many of us find this a terrible part of the battle. I told someone recently, "Know this...you are a professional woman with a career. You live a normal life. You pay your bills, raise your children, have friends, and a social life. You also have encounters with the devil. No more and no less". Gaining an understanding of this issue and accepting this truth will lead the way through the maze of spiritual warfare. Every person who comes to God will not become an intercessor. However, most of the people who suffer from this type of spiritual attack *will* become an intercessor because these attacks keep you on your knees.

Now I would like to talk about fear. I will get into how to control it in another chapter but I need to say something about it here. You will be fearful during these encounters with your adversary. He is a master at instilling fear into you. Remember that the devil is not a human, but an angelic being created by God. He has fallen from his former glory but still has great powers to frighten and influence you. Some believe that he was the musician in the heavenly hosts and it seems likely that he was definitely a part of the artistic group in the heavenlies. He is known as the Prince of the Air. He will make you fearful, and truthfully, there will always be an element of fear when you encounter any of his fallen angels. As you gain experience the fear will lessen but will always be with you. It is important to have respect for these fallen angels. You need to remember that within yourself you have *no power or ability* to stop any spiritual attack that may come against you. The *Holy Spirit* within you gives you the *authority* to bind demons and loose good spirits into your life or into the life of the person for whom you may be praying. A word of caution, be careful to talk about your spiritual encounters with Godly, mature believers who have a sound understanding. Some people do not understand and may never understand what you are going through. While there is no shame in your situation, most people being what they are will not understand. Their lack of understanding comes from a place of fear and ignorance. For whatever reason, some people never have these experiences and do not believe they are real. This includes your brothers and sisters in the Lord. So while it is important to be able to admit that you have these encounters, it is also important to be selective about the people you take into your confidence. Everyone will not understand and this could bring more pain or difficulties into your life. God will send people into your life who will help you pray about your problem.

Prayer

Heavenly Father, please send me the right prayer partners and companions who will understand the battles I am facing with my adversary. In Jesus Name.

Prayer, Prayer, and more Prayer

Let us talk about prayer. Some people have elaborate written prayers. Others say a quick word before hurrying through the day. Some people think that prayer is something formal and pious to be done only in church. What do *you* think about prayer? Do *you* know exactly what prayer is? Have you *really* prayed and *do* you pray regularly?

What *is* prayer?

"Prayer is a privilege and an obligation of the Christian and is the method we use to communicate with God. We use prayer to confess. *(1 John 1:9),* for requests *(1 Tim. 2:1-3)*, intercessions *(James 5:15)*, and thanksgiving *(Phil. 4:6)*, etc., to our holy God. We are commanded to pray *(1 Thess. 5:17)*. One must pray with a pure heart *(Psalm 66:18)*, believe in Jesus Christ *(John 14:13)*, and that the prayer be according to God's will *(1 John 5:13)"*.

Let me be clearer. Prayer defined simply is a conversation with God. In the beginning God decided to create a world full of wonderful beings. He created different types of animals, some destined to be wild, and some destined to become domesticated. He created birds and fish, too. Then he decided to create man. He wanted someone who would be able to communicate with Him on His level. Now, of course God is higher than man and it is certainly *impossible* for man to interact with God on some levels; but God created man in His image. This means that we have the intellectual attributes that make up the fullness of God. God was looking for someone to talk to. This someone would not be forced to talk to him, but would wish to do so. He wanted someone who would love Him because it was the desire of that person's heart. He did not want to force anyone to love, worship, or talk to Him. God created man a little lower than the angels *(Psalms 8:5; Hebrews*

2:7). The angels were created to serve God but they were not given the option or the choice. Angels can never be filled with the Holy Spirit. They are curious about the Holy Spirit and this great gift from God to man because they know that this joining with God is greater than anything they will ever experience *(1Peter 1: 12).* Those angels who chose to war with God were cast down to the earth out of favor with God. Their punishment waits at the end of time. But *we* have the *choice* to talk to God. We can come to him *whenever and wherever* we choose. We can pray in our hearts silently or we can pray loudly if we choose. The choice is ours to make. Prayer is a great privilege and is not to be taken lightly.

Notes

_____
_____
_____
_____
_____
_____
_____
_____
_____
_____

Do you pray?

While most of us manage small prayers or bow our heads reverently, there are those among us who do not understand the mechanics of prayer. Prayer is the most important activity in your life. You must learn *how* it is done and *why* we pray! First, most of us have been told that we should pray daily. When I was a young girl my pastor's wife, Sister Chloe Lott, told me her pastor had instructed her to pray one hour every day. She faithfully kept her eye on the clock as she maintained her hour long daily prayer vigil. This is good training and not a bad goal for the rest of us to follow. Finding an hour in one block of time is hard for many of us with the hectic lives we lead. However, we must devote a block of time for prayer to the Lord everyday. I would recommend starting with fifteen minutes to thirty minutes at a time and work up to larger blocks of time when you are comfortable with your prayers. It serves no purpose to remain on your knees with your mind wandering in a thousand directions. It is also helpful to keep a note pad and pen by your side to write down your to do list as they will invariably pop into your mind as you attempt to focus on your talk with God.

****

Worship

In a discussion about prayer I find it important to emphasize the importance of worship to God. So many times we come before the throne of God with our hearts heavy and our minds disordered. We immediately begin to pour out our troubles to the Lord. There is nothing wrong with this, but there are times when the Lord must wonder how much we love Him? *(Psalms 22:3)* The spirit of the Lord inhabits the praises of His people. If this is true then to get close to the Lord all we need to do is praise and adore Him. I am a follower of Christ. That makes me His servant. I want to worship and adore the King of Kings. I am blessed when I worship the Lord.

I am not ashamed of my worship. I approach His throne with worship.

Learning How to Approach the Throne

Worship is not the same as giving thanks. Worship lets our God know that *we know* He is high above us. God already knows that he is the Master of the Universe. *He* knows that he is Almighty and all Powerful. He would like to know that we know this. We *acknowledge* the relationship we have with Him in worship. Experience has shown me that in worship we enter the Throne Room and stand in the Holy Place. In worship we reach emotional heights. When the church comes together in a spirit of worship something wonderful happens. The Lord comes into the gathering and everyone is lifted to great heights. Healings can take place at these times because God is in the house with his people. On a smaller scale the same thing happens when you take time to worship in your daily prayer life.

The Lord's Prayer is the perfect example of how to approach the throne. In the book of Matthew Jesus gave us this example of how to pray.

Matthew 6:9-13 (KJV)

9 After this manner therefore pray ye: Our Father which art in heaven, Hallowed be thy name.

10 Thy kingdom come, Thy will be done in earth, as it is in heaven.

11 Give us this day our daily bread.

12 And forgive us our debts, as we forgive our debtors.

13 And lead us not into temptation, but deliver us from evil: For thine is the kingdom, and the power, and the glory, for ever. Amen.

So if we would like to pray in an orderly fashion it might go something like this:
1. Worship
2. Make your requests to the Lord
3. Pray for forgiveness, forgive others
4. Ask to be delivered from evil and temptation
5. End with praise and thanksgiving

The purpose of this outline is to help the new convert create order and structure in their prayer life. It is not wrong to vary the order of prayer. Prayer is not complicated and is merely a conversation between friends. Those friends happen to be God and humans. Intercessory prayer is different, more intense, and will be discussed later.

Prayer

Heavenly Father, teach me to pray. Show me the joys of coming before your throne to worship in my private prayer time. In Jesus Name.

Meditation

Meditation is an important part of your prayer life. God wants to speak to you, but if you drop to your knees and pour out your heart then jump up to run on with your life without a pause or a moment for listening you will never hear His voice. Give yourself time to listen to the voice of the Lord. Include this quiet time in every prayer session. You never know when the Lord may want to speak to you. Sometimes he speaks in an audible voice. Sometimes he impresses a verse on your mind that speaks to your soul. Sometimes you may become aware of the words of a meaningful song running through your mind after an intense prayer session. And sometimes you hear nothing. Take time to meditate on the Lord. Pick a theme for your meditation.

Choose a favorite Bible verse or something for which you are particularly thankful. Be creative. The Lord will richly reward you.

Pray Without Ceasing

1 Thessalonians 5:17; Pray without ceasing. You may be wondering how in the world I can pray all the time. That is the basic meaning of the previous verse. Certainly the Lord knows we have jobs and daily duties to occupy our minds...So just what did Paul mean when he commanded us to *"Pray without ceasing?"* The key is to keep your mind in an attitude of prayer. Listen for the voice of the Lord in the quiet moments of your day. Keep the Lord close to you no matter what happens in your life. Make a point to think about God in your free moments. *You choose* what you think about. God gave the human race the gift of choice. That means you can cast your mind back to the sermon you heard last night or this morning. You can meditate on a recent victory God gave you. There are many ways to keep an attitude of prayer. Get to know the Lord in a personal way. Read the scripture. *John 1:1; In the beginning was the Word and the Word was with God and the Word was God.* What a *powerful* statement, "*the Word was God*"! This means that every time we read the Bible and make it a part of our innermost being, we are taking God into our innermost being. What power! I am overwhelmed with the Majesty and Glory that the thought brings up! Meditate on the meaning of being filled with the Holy Spirit... I *knew* that the Lord lived inside me but one day while I was working on a busy hospital unit with my mind on my work I found out exactly what that meant. I was so busy I could barely think straight. The incident happened so fast that I did not see it coming. Sitting behind me was a doctor and two social workers. They fell into conversation and obviously they found each other interesting. Suddenly the young doctor asked, "Are either of you girls Jewish?" One of the girls said no, but the other girl made a statement that changed her future as far as God is concerned. She said, "I am converting to Judaism. I know now that Jesus is not God...He was *just a man!*"

The hair stood up on the back of my neck and in that instant although I did not turn around I physically felt the Holy Ghost lift up above my body and turn to look at the girl. I did not turn my head, but the image is deeply implanted in my mind. The Spirit of the Lord stared at her for a long moment and then settled back down into my body. It was real and I felt it physically. I was *overwhelmed* at that moment with fear for that girl. That was the first time I completely understood *exactly* what it means to be filled with the Holy Spirit. Before that time I knew that He was with me and in me, but that experience demonstrated to me exactly what He meant when he said, "*ye shall know that I am in my Father, and ye in me, and I in you*".

John 14: 16 – 20

16And I will pray the Father and he shall give you another Comforter that he may abide with you for ever;

17Even the Spirit of truth; whom the world cannot receive, because it seeth him not, neither knoweth him: but ye know him; for he dwelleth with you, and shall be in you.

18I will not leave you comfortless: I will come to you.

19Yet a little while, and the world seeth me no more; but ye see me: because I live, ye shall live also.

20 At that day ye shall know that I am in my Father, and ye in me, and I in you.

Today, I live with the understanding that God dwells within me and is *always* a part of my life. He knows exactly what I am thinking. There is never a moment when He sleeps. He is aware of all my hopes, dreams, fantasies, and other less favorable thoughts. *God knows me.* I am not unique and special. *You* can have this relationship with God as well. Devote yourself to knowing God and you will find yourself walking in heavenly places. Your relationship with God will become clear to you as you come to understand exactly how he interacts with you in the spirit. When you come to this understanding you will have barely touched the surface of your relationship with the Lord. He is in you and with you. He wants to be in communication with you every moment of your life. Pray without ceasing.

Enjoying Conversation with the Lord

Taking *pleasure* in conversation with the Lord is another phase of spiritual growth. The Lord will comfort you, supply your needs, shelter you from the adversary, and make you feel special. Knowing that the Lord will never turn me away is the greatest joy of my life. I *know* that I can receive or be anything in his presence. God does not show preference from one person to another. He does not lift up one person and reject another person. The depth of your relationship with God depends on one person...You! You set the terms of the relationship. Everyone who comes to God is on equal footing. He loves you dearly. He died for you! You are special to God. Now, that is not to say that God does not feel closer to one person or another. This is not because *He* shows preference, but because the *individual* shows preference. When *you* love to spend time in the presence of the Lord *He knows it*. He can *feel* your desire to know more about Him...or even your desire *just* to *know* Him!

Attitude is the important factor in your prayer life. Do you look forward to the time you spend in prayer? Do you dread it? Do you feel that it is an obligation that you have a hard time getting through? These are important questions that you need to answer as you pursue your spiritual growth. Once you understand that prayer time is *your* private audience with the King of Kings, and that he is available when you call you will begin to understand the magnitude of the opportunity that has been placed before you. Take pleasure in your moments alone with your God. Take joy in your journey.

Points to Ponder
1. What is prayer? (Conversation with God)
2. Worship
3. Meditation
4. Pray without ceasing
5. Enjoying your conversation with God

Take time to truly think about prayer and what it means in your life. Meditate on the facets of prayer and learn how to approach the Throne of God in the manner that will best bring you into His Presence. God loves you and wants to be on intimate terms with you. Prayer is the key to making that happen.

Notes
_____
_____
_____
_____
_____
_____
_____

Are You Ready For The Fight?

The Apostle Paul discussed spiritual warfare in the book of Ephesians *(Ephesians 6: 12).* He made it clear that warring against spiritual wickedness in high places is not only very real, but something to be expected. I believe that *every* child of God encounters spiritual wickedness directed against his or her person at some time in their life. These attacks may not be frequent. They may even be rare, but they do happen. Churches as a whole are definitely the object of spiritual attacks. Some of these encounters are quite strong and take much prayer and fasting to break the stronghold. I understand that some people are never particularly aware of being attacked by the devil or of any other spiritual attack. I do not know why some people are consistently under attack and others never seem to be touched. I *do* know that it is impossible to judge a person's walk with God by the number of spiritual attacks from the adversary. By this I mean that one is *not more* holy than another because of the depth or strength of these spiritual attacks. I can say for certain that the person who endures such attacks will become stronger spiritually. The individual who constantly battles the adversary will either become stronger or fail. This is a simple fact. There is no middle ground. I do not count hiding in the cleft of the rock as a failure. God protects us from the enemy and sometime we attack and sometime we retreat. It is all part of the battle.

    I received the Holy Ghost as a child. It was more than twenty years later that I became aware of specific directed attacks by the devil (or another fallen angel). Satan was always my adversary, but *never* like this. The dreams began suddenly. A man was talking to me. He was a dignified older gentleman with black hair with gray wings at the temple who seemed to be offering me something I wanted. I had always desired to write and this seemed to be the topic of discussion. Suddenly I realized that this was the devil. He was like nothing I had imagined. I *never* believed that the devil might *really* try to bargain with anyone for their soul. Fear struck my heart and I began to say, "Jesus, Jesus, Jesus..." over and over until I woke up drenched in sweat and terrified. Night after night these dreams continued for months. This was the first time I found myself in the arena with the devil. He had always been in the background in my life in other experiences, but I did not know how to deal with him. The truth is that I was horrified that I was in direct contact with my adversary. I was terrified. Now he was openly challenging my experience and offering me the world. I had lived for the Lord twenty-two years and was still a baby! I had *no idea* how to deal with this attack and *no confidence* to command this demon to get out of my life. I wanted to be a writer with everything in my being. I had recently published one novel with a good publishing company and was optimistic about continued success. It was during this time just after my father died that the dreams began. I found myself unable to write. After this my family life disintegrated as Satan mounted an all out attack against my marriage and my children. Events happened during these times that left permanent scars in my family. Satan has *no* love for you. *Never forget this.* He is heartless and cruel and will never stop coming once he sets his sights on you. Although I had the Holy Ghost I found myself doing things I should not have done. Life changed for me and I seemed to be walking in darkness for five years. During this time Satan stopped his active attacks in my dreams, but he kept my life in a state of chaos and devastation. Then one day I got ready for church with my children. As I was driving in my car I began thinking about the past few years and how Satan had devastated my life. I suddenly knew that no matter what had happened, God had been the *one constant* in my life. He had always been with me and I had not known it. My world had been out of kilter for many years. Right then I decided to make myself right with God. My actual thought was, "I am going home where I belong". God is my home. Then a miracle happened! I literally felt my world snap back into focus for the first time in many years. I was right with God in that moment. He accepted me with no reservations. The choices I made brought sweeping changes in my family. This did not happen over night, but the feeling that God had come back to the *surface* of my life certainly kept me in a state of awe.

Unfortunately, Satan had not forgotten me. Although I had not suffered from the dreams for several years, as soon as I began to attend church regularly and began praying again, new dreams attacked me. These dreams were different and brought fear such as I had never known. But things were different now. I was determined to learn how to fight the devil. There was no manual and no road map to follow. I had to seek the Lord and learn to pray before I could understand how to handle these spiritual attacks. I read many books about prayer and praying the word. Thetus Tenney's *Focused Light* series taught me how to use the word to overcome my adversary. I do not believe I would have survived if I had not come to understand how important praying the Word of God is in the prayer life of a Christian.

Satan continued to attack me in my dreams. One morning I got off from work and went to bed. I had been sleeping for only a few minutes when I thought someone had entered my home and was attacking me. I began to fight him off in the darkness of my room and the struggle seemed to turn me from the head of the bed to the foot of the bed. As I tried to hit my attacker I suddenly realized that he had no arms, only his hands were grabbing me. I immediately cried out, "I rebuke you Satan in the Name of Jesus Christ"! I was soundly asleep when I started talking, but when I finished the command I was sitting straight up in bed and wide awake! I had just learned another lesson about spiritual warfare. Satan *can physically attack you* if you do not take authority over him. I knew nothing about taking authority over the devil in those days. This is something I discovered later.

During the following years I continued my battle with the devil. He never left me alone for very long and I never went to bed without my sleeping Bible. I slept with it in my arms many nights for protection. I still did not understand how to deal with these attacks. I endured so many attacks in my dreams that I lost track of them. Then one night something happened within my soul. Satan attacked me again, but I rebuked him. He disappeared for a moment but came back with another dream. I rebuked him again and he came back with another dream. This third time during the night I found myself in a cave with a spotlight on me. Behind the counter in front of me were three demons (men) who seemed to be judging me. This time something wonderful happened. I looked down at my hands and realized that in my dream I was holding *my* sleeping Bible. I knew it was *my* Bible because I recognized the little tear in the cover that had come from constant use and from my sleeping with it. I raised my Bible in my hands and cried out, "I rebuke you in the Name of Jesus Christ", while pointing my Bible at them. In an instant they vanished and I awakened triumphant for the first time.

After this I became more observant of the activities in my home. I realized that many of the family quarrels had no bearing on our lives but seemed to be a result of some outside influence. I continued to ponder these thoughts for a long time. One night after a wonderful church service where the spirit moved in a mighty way, a quarrel erupted on the way home from church in which some horrible things were said that threw me back to events of my life fifteen years earlier. I was angry and realizing that this was a trick of the devil, determined in my mind to have it out with him that night. I specifically remember my adult children pulling into the driveway and asking what was the matter. I was standing on the sidewalk outside the house. I looked at them and said, "I am about to have a word with the devil, are you with me or against me"? They took one look at my face and said that of course they were with me and then ran into their apartment.

I stood outside the house in the dark for a long time trying to decide what to do. I walked up to the house and began to pray for guidance. Finally I asked the Lord to send me four warrior angels to protect me because I had something to say to the devil that might cause me to need protection. I maintained an attitude of prayer as I walked around on the back patio and waited for the angels to arrive. You see, I believe that angels are real and they must travel from where they are located to get to you. This only took a few moments and I felt comfortable. I did not see the angels, I only felt their presence. Then I began to speak." Satan, this is Sandra Mireles and I need to speak to you. I know you know me because you have been tormenting me for years. In the Name of Jesus Christ I command you to remove your familiar spirits and demons from my home. You do not belong here. *Everyone* in this house (I named every member of my family who lived there at the time) is filled with the Holy Ghost and does not belong to you. We belong to God. In the Name of Jesus Christ you will not come into my yard or on my property again!" When I stopped speaking all was silent in my neighborhood for a moment. Suddenly every dog in the area began howling. I was aware that a small white dog was coming toward me barking. I rebuked it and it went back into the ditch and did not emerge. I still have the image of that small dog in my mind. I often wonder if that pitiful visible image of the spirit is what had been tormenting my family. I learned a valuable lesson that night. After that I did not suffer from demonic attacks in my home for the remainder of the years I lived in that house (about four).

A few months later I was going through a trial and began writhing in the bed speaking in tongues and tossing and turning. I was in the middle of an attack from another demon. This time it was different. When my husband awakened me I immediately cried out, "It is okay...He is not in the house...He is not in the house!" I had a vivid image of the demon in my dreams standing across the fence at the back of my house shouting at me. Although the experience was unpleasant it confirmed to me that we can take authority over the devil if we have the strength to do it.

I do not pretend to know or understand why I or the other people I know who have similar experiences are been singled out for such attacks. Many times I have puzzled over the obvious and very real attacks I have suffered in my life. I still have no answers as to why.

One thing I do know is that they are very real and *not* imagined. These attacks took place over a period of twenty years. I learned a lot from them and today I hope to help someone else by describing the various and numerous attacks that I endured from the devil. I also want to offer hope. As spirit filled believers we have the *right* to rebuke any adversary who dares to enter our home and attack us personally. The scripture is very clear on this point. *Mark 16: 17* list the signs of a believer. One of these signs is that they will cast out demons.

Notes

Spiritual Warfare

I do not advise *any* layman to challenge the devil without due cause. In other words, if Satan comes after you; you have the right to fight back. **I DO NOT RECOMMEND TO ANYONE TO BECOME A DEMON HUNTER.** I do not advise any layman to practice exorcism. Leave that to the professionals. It is foolish and unwise. That is not the focus or purpose of this discussion. My hope is that someone who is suffering from oppression will receive the tools to live an overcoming life. I did not enter the arena of spiritual warfare by choice. I never considered the idea of battling the devil to be romantic, interesting, or tantalizing. I was drawn into the arena by personal attacks in my life that left me with a choice: fight or die. I chose life...

My experience was one of being attacked by my adversary for many years of my life. This is one type of spiritual warfare. When under attack we have the right to defend our families and our selves from this bitter foe. Know this; you **can** through the *Power of God* overcome the devil and find peace. This peace may be hard won. This is an uneasy feeling because after you enter the arena where these spiritual battles are fought you grow spiritually and will be able to observe others in the middle of a fight. You will recognize what is happening. You will become acutely aware of the spiritual forces around you. You will instinctively know when these spirits try to come into your home or into the life of one of your family members. Through prayer and travail you will become more sensitive to the spiritual world. At times you may know when something is happening before it happens. Sometimes you will be very hesitant to re-enter the arena. Spiritual battles are not easy and they are in fact exhausting. Determination and strength of purpose is key to winning over your enemy. You already have the power. You received power the moment you were filled with the Holy Spirit. You must have *absolute* faith in God that He will deliver you and then proceed with determination and strength of purpose. Your prayers will become longer and longer. You will enter a new dimension with God where you have never walked before.

The writing of this book has taken me back into the arena. Satan fought me on every side. I suffered physical and emotional attacks from the moment I started work this book. My adversary does not want *anyone* to have the tools to take the fight to him. It is important to understand that it is *not enough* to know how to deal with the devil. **Never** assume that the power to overcome your adversary is innate and comes from your strength of will. This fight can only be won by a person who is filled with the spirit because it is the *spirit of God* within that gives one the power to face the adversary and win.

Getting Ready for the Fight

It is important to know what is ahead if you choose to engage the devil on his terms. By this I mean specifically that there is a price to be paid for engaging the enemy. This type of spiritual warfare may come because you see that a loved one, your pastor, or your church is under attack. The nature of the problem will decide how eager you are to join the battle. Now, you may ask why would I *not* choose to engage the enemy if I know I can be successful? The main reason for avoiding the fight is weariness. There *will be* times when you are stretched so thin by the cares of your life that you may believe you *cannot* engage your adversary in a head on all out fight for survival! We are all still human and experience our own inadequacies and other personal difficulties. None of us exist in a vacuum. All of our lives are impacted by the people we live with and who are around us. Your life may have become so traumatic that you are hiding in the cleft of the rock and hanging on for dear life. There is no shame in this. Many circumstances in life can wear you down to the point that you feel there is no fight left in you. At these times you must allow the Holy Spirit to be your Comforter and let the Lord to shelter you in his wing until you have the strength to return to the battle.

If you decide to join the fight there are some things you must do. (1) You must pray (2) You must pray (3) You must pray. I cannot *stress enough* the importance of readying your mind to be an intercessor in this manner.

Your adversary has no need to be a mind reader to find your weak points. These fallen angels have been around a long time and they are students of human nature. They can observe you for a while and make very good guesses as to what you are thinking. It is not easy to hide your thoughts from these demons. They speculate and go to work planning their attack. If you desire to have private conversation with God, ask Him. Many times I have requested a private audience with the Lord and asked that the ears of my adversary be closed so they cannot hear what I have to discuss. I firmly believe that the Lord places a hedge around us in these times.

In the times of spiritual attack your only hope is to strengthen yourself with prayer and fasting so that you stir up the gift that is within you and are able to resist the fiery darts of the enemy who hurls them at you. Before you back away in fear, understand that this is a *Great Hope.* Prayer and fasting can and will overcome **any and all** traps of the devil. It is important not to be overcome with fear, but to recognize that the spirit of God that is within you is greater than the spirit of the adversary that is in the world. It is true that a war is taking place, but it is a war you can win with the proper tools and determination. You will go forth in the Name of the Lord.

Points to Ponder:
1. Do I believe in spiritual attacks?
2. You *may* or *may not* be the subject of spiritual attacks
3. Whether or not you are the target of spiritual attacks has no bearing on the quality of your walk with God.
4. Spiritual attacks occur for no reason that you may be able to discern.
5. If I am the object of a spiritual attack, how will I deal with it?
6. Will I be able to recognize a spiritual attack when it comes?
7. The power to overcome the adversary comes from God. Within ourselves we have no power.
8. I can have private conversation with God without my adversary eavesdropping.

Ephesians 6:16
Above all, taking the shield of faith, wherewith ye shall be able to quench all the **fiery darts** *of the wicked.*

It is important to understand that it is not enough to **know how** to deal with the devil. **Never** assume that the power to overcome your adversary is innate and comes from your strength of will. This fight **can only** be won by a person who is filled with the spirit because it is the spirit of God within that gives one the power to face the adversary and win.

Dealing with Fear

Satan uses the weapon of fear to inflict his pain on many of us. Fear can enter into the heart to paralyze us and make us afraid of our very shadow. If allowed to operate unchecked fear can take over your life and devastate you. For example, many years ago my family moved into an apartment complex and immediately I became aware of an irrational fear of being alone in my bedroom. I could be alone in any room in the apartment, but could never sleep in the bedroom alone. Many times I was uncomfortable even when my husband was in the room. I did not want to talk about it but this fear haunted me for several months. I was in an early phase of my learning process about spiritual attacks and had no idea what caused me to feel like this.

I tried many things to make this fear dissipate. Unfortunately, none of them worked. I searched the scriptures for advice about fear. I learned a lot. Here are some verses to use when your adversary brings fear into your life.

Deuteronomy 31:8 And the LORD, he it is that doth go before thee; he will be with thee, he will not fail thee, neither forsake thee: fear not, neither be dismayed

Romans 8:15 For ye have not received the spirit of bondage again to fear; but ye have received the Spirit of adoption, whereby we cry, Abba, Father.

2 Timothy 1:7 For God hath not given us the spirit of fear; but of power, and of love, and of a sound mind.

1 John 4:18 There is no fear in love; but perfect love casteth out fear: because fear hath torment. He that feareth is not made perfect in love.

Revelation 2:10 Fear none of those things which thou shalt suffer: behold, the devil shall cast some of you into prison, that ye may be tried; and ye shall have tribulation ten days: be thou faithful unto death, and I will give thee a crown of life.

Isaiah 54:17 *No weapon that is formed against thee shall prosper; and every tongue that shall rise against thee in judgment thou shalt condemn. This is the heritage of the servants of the LORD, and their righteousness is of me, saith the LORD.*

    I found myself spending more and more time in prayer. I had never prayed directly against the tricks of the devil in the past. As I look back I realize that I spent most of my early years taking baby steps in the Lord. I lived in fear that my adversary would look in my direction. I did not understand that I had within me the *Power* to stop Satan right in his tracks. That does not mean that Satan will not come back. That does not mean that the fight will end forever. It means that *we are able to control our environment through the power of God*!

Getting back to my experience, one day I could no longer tolerate the fear and uneasy feeling I felt in that bedroom. I began to talk to the Lord about it and before I knew it I found myself crying out to the Lord to cleanse my apartment from the spirit of evil and fear that had seemingly bound me. Once the dam burst the words broke forth in a shower of pleas to God to cleanse the apartment of this fear. As I prayed I begged the Lord to cast the devil from my apartment, the apartment above me, and before I knew it I was asking for all the apartments round about where I lived to be cleansed in the name of Jesus Christ. The flood gates had opened and I was able to focus my thoughts in the exact direction I wanted them to go.

Within days the family living directly above our apartment moved without warning. They had been living in the apartment before we came and had remained there for more than a year. When that family moved out of the apartment the fear went with them. I do not know what type of people they were or how they lived. I do know that evil lived in the bedroom just above my apartment. When they left the fear went with them. I did not have that problem again as long as I lived in that apartment. God delivered me from the fear and the presence of evil these people had entertained. This was the beginning of my journey into the arena of *spiritual warfare.*

Points to Ponder

1. Think about fear and how you personally handle fear in your life.

2. *II Timothy 1:7 For God hath not given us the spirit of fear; but of power, and of love, and of a sound mind.*

3. Remember that God is not the author of fear and wants you to live with perfect love.

Notes

_____
_____
_____
_____
_____

Inner Conflict

God created us in His image. He made us sentient beings with the ability to laugh, love, think, make wrong choices, understand right choices, and understand that at some point in our journey we will die. These qualities make us who we are. So it is not surprising that we should spend a great deal of time agonizing over past or future actions. We were created with a sinful nature (*Romans 8*). This sinful nature creates great conflict within us. I recommend reading Romans chapters 7-8 in the New International Version for clarity and a better understanding of how sin tries to control our minds. Our sinful nature is an integral part of our makeup and is not something we can toss out. We were born with a sinful nature and it is part of the human condition. So if we cannot get rid of it, what are we to do?

Romans 7: 21 *So I find this law at work: When I want to do good, evil is right there with me. 22 For in my inner being I delight in God's law; 23 but I see another law at work in the members of my body, waging war against the law of my mind and making me a prisoner of the law of sin at work within my members. 24 What a wretched man I am! Who will rescue me from this body of death? 25 Thanks be to God—through Jesus Christ our Lord! (New International Version)*

This conflict in the innermost being is not new. Paul felt the need to talk about it in his letter to the Romans. The Romans could not understand why with the best will in the world they found themselves unable to keep from sinning. They loved the Lord just like you and me. And yet there were times when they failed to meet their own personal standard of right and wrong. We today continue to be likewise afflicted with these inner conflicts. Satan uses these conflicts against us to suit his purposes.

Satan loves to use our inadequacies against us. Sometimes these mistakes are imaginary, but Satan magnifies them and makes it appear as if the whole world knows our shameful secrets. When you are in the middle of a spiritual attack you *may* feel as if the whole world is against you. Satan uses every weapon in his arsenal against you. He will take *every* word you say and twist it into something you never intended. He will make your *most innocent actions* seem to be something sinister and ugly. It is during these times when you must grow spiritually and examine your actions accurately. Think about your words, your thoughts, and your actions. If you know in your heart that you had no wrong intentions when you spoke or thought...it could be the devil accusing you.

You may find yourself at odds with yourself or others around you. You may find yourself reacting negatively to sermons or innocent comments made by others you respect. You may have mixed feelings as to *why* you reacted to badly to a sermon or part of the sermon. In your heart you know that this is not the way you usually think about things. *What causes this reaction?* Again it is important to understand how far the devil is willing to go to turn you away from your path. If Satan can make you doubt your leader, he has achieved a great victory. If Satan can make you doubt the integrity of your church family he has achieved a great victory. If Satan can make you doubt yourself, the victory is even greater. Once you begin to doubt yourself it will not be long before you begin to doubt your leaders and others around you. When doubt comes in the door, faith goes out the window.

Ephesians 3:16 That he would grant you, according to the riches of his glory, to be strengthened with might by his Spirit in the inner man; (King James Version)

God wants to ease your burdens. He understands your weakness and humanity. It is good to remember that many times we judge ourselves more harshly than the Lord *Himself.* That is not to say that God excuses sin. God offered a remedy for sin through the death of His Son Jesus Christ. God understands your human faults and frailties. He knows there will be failures. It is part of the human experience. He made a way of escape and does not sit in judgment every time you slip up. When we confess our faults He is ready and willing to forgive you.

*1 John 1:9 If we **confess our sins**, he is faithful and just to forgive us **our sins**, and to cleanse us from all unrighteousness.*

Romans 8: 31 What, then, shall we say in response to this? If God is for us, who can be against us?... 38For I am convinced that neither death nor life, **neither angels nor demons***, neither the present nor the future, nor any powers, 39neither height nor depth, nor anything else in all creation, will be able to separate us from the love of God that is in Christ Jesus our Lord. (New International Version)*

    The beautiful thing about living for the Lord is that nothing can ever separate us from the love of God. That means fallen ***angels or demons!***

    It is normal for you to feel conflicted about your life at times. There will be times when you doubt your abilities. Turn to the Word of God for help when these times of conflict come. God will offer you comfort and strength. Reach out to God in prayer to find a bridge across the difficulties you are facing in your life. Never doubt your place in God's plan. Remember that the Lord promised never to leave or forsake you. That is a big promise. We are never alone! It is up to you to take Him at His word. Believe that his promises are true and that you are never alone. When you are able to take hold of the great promise and believe that the Lord wants to be everything to you, you will have learned a big lesson. He will never leave you or forsake you. It is a promise.

Points to Ponder

1. What causes inner conflict? How do I deal with it?
2. Romans 7 (Read) to understand that *we all* have the tendency to sin in spite of our best efforts to live right.
3. Romans 8: 31 *What, then, shall we say in response to this? If God is for us, who can be against us?... 38 For I am convinced that neither death nor life, neither angels nor demons, neither the present nor the future, nor any powers, 39 neither height nor depth, nor anything else in all creation, will be able to separate us from the love of God that is in Christ Jesus our Lord. (New International Version)*

4. Make a list of scriptures to use when Satan comes against you. Look up scriptures about fear, faith, love, etc.

Notes
_____
_____
_____
_____
_____
_____
_____
_____
_____
_____
_____
_____
_____
_____
_____
_____
_____
_____
_____
_____

Absolute Trust

Walking by faith is not easy. Paul explained to the church at Corinth, *(For we walk by faith, not by sight: 2 Corinthians 5:7)* the importance of living and working in a spirit of faith. There will be times when you will not be able to see the way before you. It is during these times that you must develop absolute trust in your *experience* and your *walk* with God.

So how do you develop absolute trust? This is not an easy one. Confidence in God is *usually* developed over time as you find Him faithful in your daily life. It is not impossible for a new believer to have absolute trust but it might not be easy. Jesus said that you must become as a little child in your understanding. Think about it...children are honest and sincere in their interaction with other people. They tend to believe everything they are told until they learn they cannot trust you.

Matthew18:3

*And said, Verily I say unto you, Except ye be **converted**, and become as **little children**, ye shall not enter into the kingdom of heaven.*

God expects us to believe in Him to the uttermost! He wants you to come to Him secure in the knowledge that He hears you and *wants* to supply your needs.

Trusting God to supply your needs, both physical and spiritual, does not mean that you have the right to expect God to say yes to every prayer request you make. The book of James makes it clear that the Lord will answer our prayers as long as we pray according to His *will*. This means that you should not expect God to behave like a grandfather waiting to grant your every wish. That is not going to happen. If this is your reality and vision of your relationship with God, you are destined for disappointment.

Your relationship with God requires you to understand that there *will be* times when your prayer receives a negative answer. Jesus promised to provide all your *needs*! He promised to help you carry your burdens, and He promised be your Comforter. Your responsibility is to continue to have absolute trust when your prayers are answered with a resounding "No"! This will not be easy. In fact, it will sometimes be very hard to understand God's plan for your life. It is during these times when you will walk blindly; not knowing what is ahead for you. While it is true that trust comes with time and experience, it is also possible to *choose* to trust God. We make choices every day of our lives. I am talking about the kind of trust that makes you absolutely certain that God will make a way for whatever your *need* may be! I am talking about knowing in your innermost being that God is on your side and that He is aware of you as an individual and is taking a personal interest in your situation. This kind of trust is what you display when you get to the end of your rope and make a knot and hold on for dear life, never doubting. Sometimes you trust the Lord when you stubbornly dig in your heels and refuse to give place to the devil no matter what the circumstance in your life.

Coming to the point of *absolute trust* in the face of disaster *requires* you to make choices. There will be times in your life when the needs outweigh your resources. Sickness, death, poverty, loss, are examples of needs that require an extra measure of faith and trust. Things will come into your life over which you have no control. The way you deal with these events will make or break you in your walk with God.

During these times of walking by faith you will be besieged by your adversary whose sole purpose is to cause you to lose your faith, your trust, and stray from the path you have set for yourself. Understand this; you *do not* walk alone. Every spirit filled believer has the Comforter, which is *God within you*. This means that you are never alone. God wants you to live an overcoming life. It is up to you to make that happen.

Jeremiah 17: 7-10

7 Blessed is the man that trusteth in the LORD, and whose hope the LORD is.
8 For he shall be as a tree planted by the waters, and that spreadeth out her roots by the river, and shall not see when heat cometh, but her leaf shall be green; and shall not be careful in

the year of drought, neither shall cease from yielding fruit.

9 The heart is deceitful above all things, and desperately wicked: who can know it?

10 I the LORD search the heart, I try the reins, even to give every man according to his ways, and according to the fruit of his doings.

Walking by Faith requires you to forget what your heart tells you. As we just read in Jeremiah, "...The heart is deceitful and desperately wicked, who can know it?" There will be times when you will not be able to rely on your heart. When your world is in chaos and your life is falling to pieces around you it is important to have the tools in place and a plan of escape ready. When your adversary accuses you and laughs in your face because your life has blown up in your face you need to know what to do. You need to know how to *walk by faith, not by sight!*

Absolute trust, confidence in God, and walking by faith are all parts of the same quality. Acquiring these qualities and allowing them to operate in your life is a choice. As you walk with the Lord you set the terms of your relationship. God will offer you understanding, wisdom, knowledge, and many more abilities to lighten your load. You will not wake up one morning and discover that you have absolute trust, confidence in God, and are magically able to walk by faith with no trouble. God does not bestow these qualities in your life. These qualities, or abilities, however you term them, are developed by the individual who seeks to serve the Lord with his or her whole heart. You develop these abilities in your life through periods of pain, difficulty, and hurts that come your way.

Now...*absolute trust* also requires you to trust God when He does *not* heal your loved one, change your financial circumstances when you think he should do it (on your time schedule), or *save* your lost loved one. Absolute trust and confidence in God is necessary when your loved one dies and you were certain God meant to heal him or her. When a loved one fails you and you want God to change his or her mind and make him behave, you must continue to have absolute trust in God when it does not happen. It is important to understand that the great contract between God and the human race guarantees every person the right to make decisions. That means that God will never force one person to change their behavior or mind about anything, no matter how hard you plead with Him to do it! God's contract with the human race demands that all beings be allowed to make individual choices.

One of the devil's greatest joys is throwing in your face that God has let you down and failed you because he did not restore your marriage or your relationship with an estranged child or sibling. It is up to you to fall back on your confidence in God and have absolute trust that He knows what He is doing. He knows the end from the beginning. God will woo every individual but he *will not* force anyone into His service. It is all about choice. Understanding that your relationship with God is *all about choice* is the beginning of your transformation and development of your ability to have confidence in God and absolute trust.

Finally, it is impossible to have absolute trust in God if you doubt your walk every time things do not go your way. You must make up your mind that you are not turning your back on the Lord when He does not give you the answer you want. No one ever gets everything they ask from the Lord. God reserves to himself the right to say no and the right to answer on His time schedule. Make up your mind today that you are a servant of the Most High. Decide right now that no matter what happens in your life you are going to trust the Lord, and even the **thought** of turning back will never enter your mind. Trust God.

Points to Ponder
1. Absolute trust
2. Confidence in God
3. Walking by faith, not by sight
4. Personal choice, the great contract between God and the human race.
5. Understanding what God will and will not do
6. Learning that absolute trust means trusting God when things go right as well as when things go wrong and you wonder what happened.
7. Make a decision now to serve the Lord and never think about turning back.

Prayer
Father, my hope is in you. I have made up my mind that I will never turn back to sin and cease from following you. Help me to learn to have absolute trust when my life is not going as planned. In Jesus Name.

Spiritual Warfare A Handbook

Notes:

Winning the War!

Satan will never give up the battle. When you understand that the battle is ongoing you will be better able to define to your own satisfaction the *meaning* of winning the war. The ongoing battle between the fallen angels and the saints will never end until Jesus calls you away through death or in the Rapture of the Church. While you continue to exist on earth you will have difficulties with your adversary. Jesus told his disciples to "take up your cross daily and follow me". Modern day Christians must also pick up their cross daily and follow the Lord. This means that although we succeeded yesterday, today is a new day and therefore we go back to the fight.

We win battles. Sometimes we are wounded...but we do not give up! Learning to manage spiritual attacks is an ongoing process. Amazingly enough the harder the fight, the stronger you become. Satan and all the fallen angels have one mission and one purpose that stated plainly, is to destroy people. He wants to destroy your life on earth as well as prevent you from reaching heaven in eternity. He will do anything within his power to keep you from unity with the Lord. As Christians we tend to take the view that our adversary dedicates himself *only* to the destruction of all Christians. Nothing could be further from the truth. Many people who are not professing Christians do battle with the adversary regularly. We must understand that our adversary hates *all people* everywhere. He will always hate the human race and will use all his power to destroy every one of us. That includes believers and non-believers alike. Nothing pleases our adversary more than watching a child of God fail.

Many believers and *all* unbelievers are ill-equipped for the battle and usually end up taking the worst of it. Some unbelievers appeal to intercessors they know to pray God's protection over them. This helps for a time, but is never a long term or permanent solution.

The Lord does allow for Godly intercession, and he allows prayer warriors to stand in the gap for others. However, the time will come when every person must take up the fight for themselves. It is inevitable. The only certain means of battling the devil requires a spirit filled individual who puts on the whole armor of God to venture forth in prayer in the Name of Jesus Christ.

Ephesians 6

10 Finally, my brethren, be strong in the Lord, and in the power of his might.

11 Put on the whole armour of God that ye may be able to stand against the wiles of the devil.

12 For we wrestle not against flesh and blood, but against principalities, against powers, against the rulers of the darkness of this world, against spiritual wickedness in high places.

13 Wherefore take unto you the whole armour of God that ye may be able to withstand in the evil day, and having done all, to stand.

14 Stand therefore, having your loins girt about with truth, and having on the breastplate of righteousness;

15 And your feet shod with the preparation of the gospel of peace;

16 Above all, taking the shield of faith, wherewith ye shall be able to quench all the fiery darts of the wicked.

17 And take the helmet of salvation, and the sword of the Spirit, which is the word of God:

18 Praying always with all prayer and supplication in the Spirit, and watching thereunto with all perseverance and supplication for all saints;

How can we expect to win the war against a powerful and wicked enemy? There is a way this can be done.

1. Know Your Adversary

Knowledge is power and when we learn all we can about our adversary we are able to defend ourselves and our loved ones from the fiery darts of the enemy. So what do we know about our adversary?

    a. He is a liar

    b. He is a deceiver

    c. He is the accuser of the brethren

d. He hates you

e. He is a destroyer of souls

f. He will never stop attacking

g. He creates confusion

Do some research and see if you can discover more traits of your adversary. It is important to know exactly what you are up against. Satan attacks every individual in a manner that is unique to that person. My pain is not the same as yours. You may or may not be sensitive in the same area. You may not have the same weakness that I possess. Know your adversary. Do a retrospective of your life and consider your successes as well as your failures. Do you see a pattern? Each of us is accountable for our own choices in life, but with a bit of research you may discover weak points where your enemy influenced your actions and choices in the past. This will give you a foundation on which to build a new and overcoming life.
Ephesians 4: 27 Neither give place to the devil.
Take time to read chapter 4 in Ephesians. This chapter offers a window into the actions and behaviors of a Christian. We should never allow sin into our lives. Sin

makes us weak and vulnerable to attacks from the adversary. When you allow yourself to sin and feel comfortable, you are offering the devil a position in your life where he will take advantage of the opportunity to destroy you and everyone around you. Do not allow the devil to live in your life. "Neither give place to the devil". Many years ago I heard a story:

> A young man was walking down a country road in the heart of winter. The trees had lost their leaves and snow was falling down in a slow dance. As the young man hurried toward home and the warmth of his fire he came upon a snake that was nearly frozen. The snake could barely croak out a plea, "Help me…please help me". The young man was a bit nervous, but he felt sorry for the frozen snake and picked it up and carried it home with him. He put the snake down by the fire where it warmed up and soon began to eye the young man as its prey. He coiled himself to strike and bit the young man who cried out, "I saved you! I brought you home with me! You would be dead if I hadn't saved you!".

As the young man fell to the floor, he watched the snake slither away. He could just hear a hiss, "You *knew* I was a snake when you picked me up".
Author unknown.

Satan is exactly like this snake. He cannot be trusted. You cannot turn your back on him, and you can never feel safe when he is around. You know he cannot be trusted so you must never feel comfortable in his presence. Just when you think all is well he will strike you with the ferocity of the coiled snake!

2. Know Your Weapons

You do not need physical weapons in your fight against your adversary. Paul makes very clear that the weapons of our warfare are not carnal... In other words we use spiritual weapons to fight spiritual battles.

2 Corinthians 10:3-5 (King James Version)

*3 For though we walk in the flesh, **we do not war after the flesh:** 4 (For the weapons of our warfare*

are not carnal, but mighty through God to the pulling down of strong holds ;) 5 Casting down imaginations and every high thing that exalteth itself against the knowledge of God, and bringing into captivity every thought to the obedience of Christ;

Notes

_____
_____
_____
_____
_____
_____
_____
_____
_____
_____
_____
_____

What Are These Spiritual Weapons?

Jesus Christ conquered Satan, death, hell, and the grave by his death on the cross of Calvary. Satan was defeated at that very moment. However, what we fail to understand is that the spirit of destruction and hatred was reinforced in that moment. His determination to destroy the human race and prove his superiority to God has never wavered. The spirit of Lucifer and the spirit of the other fallen angels remain in the world to continue the war against God. In spite of the fact that Satan knows he is defeated he will not give in. He will not admit to himself or anyone else that Jesus Christ won on the cross. The Father of Lies tells his biggest lie to himself. Let us move on to the weapons we have at our disposal.

   a. The Holy Spirit (Power)
   b. The birthright gift bestows to the believer the ability to cast out devils.
   c. The whole armor of God

13Therefore put on the full armor of God, so that when the day of evil comes, you may be able to stand your ground, and after you have done everything, to stand. 14Stand firm then, with the **belt of truth buckled around your waist, with the breastplate of righteousness in place, 15and with your feet fitted with the readiness that comes from the gospel of peace.** 16In addition to all this, take up the **shield of faith**, with which you can extinguish all the flaming arrows of the evil one. 17Take the **helmet of salvation and the sword of the Spirit, which is the word of God.** Ephesians 6:13-17 (NIV).

d. The Name of Jesus (Plead the blood of Jesus)

Now I know you are thinking, "It is one thing to have this arsenal at your disposal and an entirely different thing to know how to use it"; and you are right! Understanding how to face your adversary is a process. However, you can learn how to do it!

Jesus left us complete instructions as to how to deal with our adversary. There is no magical mumbo-jumbo. No chants or other great mystery to comprehend! There is only the plain truth and belief. Jesus said, "Only believe". Mark 5: *35 While he yet spake, there came from the ruler of the synagogue's house certain which said, Thy daughter is dead: why troublest thou the Master any further? 36As soon as Jesus heard the word that was spoken, he saith unto the ruler of the synagogue,* ***Be not afraid, only believe.***

These words offer the key to your spiritual path. Believe. This word is the crux of the discussion. No one can achieve anything in the Kingdom of God without this crucial element. *Hebrews 11: 6 But without faith it is impossible to please **him**: for he that cometh to God* *must **believe** that he is, and that he is a **rewarder** of them that **diligently seek him**.*

If you have been born again, or filled with the Holy Spirit, you are already a believer. Now you must build on the foundation you have already established. The *Enemy* of your soul will never cease to question your belief system. He will mock you, torment you, and whisper every kind of thought into your ears. It is up to you to refuse to *entertain* these notions. Recognize that you are an intelligent person. When evil thoughts enter your head, question the source. Question your own motivations, and intentions. Satan loves to sow enmity among the church family. Sometimes he puts a lot of effort into it. We as a people must not allow these thoughts to take root in our minds and develop into something God would not approve. Keep a repentant spirit and be willing to question your own inner thoughts and motivations. The truth is that sometimes we have feelings and thoughts that seem to be right, but after consideration are not right. It is up to the individual to make him or herself accountable for their very thoughts before they can be put into action.

When you have questioned yourself and searched your heart and still believe that something is really not right. Then you must bring these issues before the *Throne of God* during your prayer time. Be honest and open allowing the Lord to speak to your heart. Seek His face openly and honestly. God will hear and direct you. Believe. I cannot stress enough the importance of **believing** that God will hear you and answer you!

Belief and faith go hand in hand. Let us examines some definitions of the word.

> *—Synonyms assurance. Belief, certainty, conviction refer to acceptance of, or confidence in, an alleged fact or body of facts as true or right without positive knowledge or proof.* **Belief** *is such acceptance in general.* **Certainty** *indicates unquestioning belief and positiveness in one's own mind that something is true: I know this for a certainty.* **Conviction** *is settled, profound, or earnest belief that something is right: a conviction that a decision is just.*

Dictionary.com Unabridged (v 1.1)Based on the Random House Unabridged Dictionary, © Random House, Inc. 2006.

I am taking my definition of faith directly from the Word of God. *Hebrews 11:1 Now faith is the substance of things hoped for, the evidence of things not seen.* So we see that faith is envisioning something that has not happened and accepting in your mind without doubting that it will happen. The whole Christian experience is based on belief and faith. Again I refer you back to Hebrews 11:6. Know that we must have faith and believe that our God is a rewarder of those who seek him earnestly and diligently. As soul winners we need to be mindful that this element of faith and belief does not always come easy to those we want to win to the Lord. The path to salvation is one that leads through doubt, misunderstanding, counting the cost, unbelief, belief and faith.

For those of us joined in the battle, it is sometimes difficult to maintain our faith when hope seems gone. Many years ago I heard a sermon that reflected the importance of making up your mind to hold on to the Lord before you find yourself inside the storm. This idea took hold of my heart and I have pondered for many years what it means. The basic thought is to make up one's mind as to how one will behave in trouble before the trouble comes. This is a profound suggestion and has stood the test of time. We as a people can be certain that troublesome times are upon us. There is no doubt that Satan will bring pain and difficulties into our lives. But the light in the darkness is the choice that we make before the trouble and difficulty comes. If our minds are set on the Lord and it has already been decided that no matter what comes our way we will trust the Lord, there is **no way** your adversary can move you, shake you, or make you fall down.

My mother was diagnosed with cancer last year. It was frightening and the family was rightly distressed. I had the opportunity to spend time alone with Mother the night before she had to go to the hospital for her surgery. We talked about what was happening and then I told her, "Mother, we always knew this day might come and we are prepared for it. We are going to do what we have always done. We are going to depend on the Lord". At 76 years of age my mother had to go through six surgeries within 4 weeks. It was a dark time, but not once did I ever doubt that God was going to raise her up. She came home from the hospital and within four months she was up and around again. She gave up her walker and learned to walk and regained her strength. Mother never doubted that God was on her side. Mother's appendix burst four days before she entered the hospital for the first time. She never ran a temperature and was feeling fine when she went to the hospital for her surgery! What a miracle. The doctors found cysts on her ovaries in the scans before the surgeries. There was no doubt of their existence and yet when they got inside to do the surgery there were no cysts. God had removed them! When doctors found cancerous cells in her body six months later it was a miracle because there was no mass to be seen and they accidentally found the cancer cells during a routine examination. These cancer cells had been in her body all along and had not grown at all during the previous months. At present Mother is undergoing chemotherapy and God is still faithful. Mother knows that her situation could be much worse. She has not suffered the full and most devastating affects of chemotherapy. She is tired but not sick all the time. During the months of this treatment Mother has not lost her hair but it had thinned out from the anesthesia she took last year. In fact her hair that she lost after her many surgeries has begun to grow back *while* she is receiving her chemotherapy. Mother asked God to let her hair grow back. He did. God is faithful. We as a family decided to believe like David of old, Psalms 20:*7 Some trust in chariots, and some in horses: but we will remember the name of the LORD our God.* We know that at some point the end may come, but for Mother it is a win win situation. If she goes on to meet her reward, she will be with the Lord. If she stays here she will be with her family. She has decided to put her trust and faith in the Lord.

My nephew spent three years in the army and in the last year of his service was posted overseas to serve in the Iraq War. As a family we decided that we would not allow the war to claim his life. We bound together before God in a declared fast and prayer every day for the entire time he spent in the war. Every member of the family who was able took a day and he was covered round the clock every day for over a year until he came back from the service. Our prayer was for God to keep him alive, but also to return him to us with his mind intact as well. God placed angels on guard around him during his time there. He told of miracles that happened when he as a medic ran through bullets to rescue a soldier who had been seriously wounded. The soldier died in his arms but he did not receive a scratch! God is faithful. My nephew has been home for a year now and he said to me once, "Aunt Sandra, I don't understand it! Most of my friends are really messed up, but I am not. I don't get it". I told him that his family had prayed specifically for his mental health during his time in the service. He was amazed. God is faithful.

God performed miracles for our family during our year long commitment to fast and pray. However, we did not get away without a scratch. Satan was angry about the inroads we made into his territory in that evil land. Members of my family involved in the fast have been attacked by the devil. One of my family members was stalked for two years by a demon that tried to frighten her, threatened her in her dreams, and appeared to her while she was awake in an effort to intimidate her. He told her he meant to attack her and her family because he had been run out of Baghdad. Once again as a family we bound together in a fast and prayed together to bind this spirit and cast it into outer darkness. She has not been troubled by this spirit again. Other members of my family have been attacked as well. And yet, it appears that God had great victories In Iraq during the year long fast and prayer commitment by the family. We may never know all the victories that are achieved when we commit ourselves to spiritual warfare. When we pray and fast, God uses the power from our joint effort to pull down strongholds in the enemy camp. I take great consolation in knowing that even if we must continue to battle our adversary in retribution for the protection we obtained for our relative. *That* particularly enemy *was* run out of Baghdad! Praise be to God!

Notes

_____

_____

_____

_____

Prayer

Father, I thank you for the protection you give us and our loved ones when we pray to you in faith believing. Teach us the value of prayer and fasting. In Jesus Name.

Examples of Spiritual Encounters

In this chapter I mean to give you some true life encounters with the devil. Each one is true and really happened. Names have been left out to offer privacy to the individuals, but I am acquainted with the facts and know them to be absolutely true. The purpose for giving these first person encounters is to make you understand what can happen to you and that you can overcome these attacks.

1. This is my own personal experience. I drove up to my mother's home many years ago to pick her up for an outing. As I waited in the driveway for her I became aware that there was a disturbance in my spiritual environment. I have difficulty

explaining to others what I mean, but sometimes my *spiritual antennae* just go up and I feel something happening around or near me. Next to the garage I became aware that a very tall spirit was waiting. He was as tall as the garage roof and was looking directly at me. I realized that he was aware that I knew he was there and yet he did not attempt to interfere with my business at all. I felt him look directly at me and I stared back at him. This was the first time I understood that the spirits have assignments and at this moment I was not the intended target. He had no interest in me for the moment. I mentioned the visit of this spirit to my mother and she stored it in her mind for later thought. This incident happened during the 1990's, and was part of my journey toward understanding the spiritual world.

2. Recently my grandson spent the night with us and came home around 11:30 pm. He went to bed fairly early. I sometimes have trouble sleeping and was napping in the recliner in my bedroom. Some time later I began to dream that I was awake in my bedroom in the very recliner where I was at that moment sleeping. I saw a

short Hispanic man walk through the wall adjacent to the bed where my grandson was sleeping. I realized that this man was in fact a minor demon or familiar spirit. His eyes darted about and he appeared to be in a panic. After a moment he pulled himself together and walked forward to stand directly in front of me in the recliner where I was sleeping. He had a smirk on his face that I can only describe as false bravado. I was so surprised by his appearance and the fact that he had presented himself to me that without thinking I cried out, "I rebuke you in the Name of Jesus Christ. Get out of this house"! He was gone in the instant and I was awake when I finished speaking. It was exactly 02:17 am. I found myself puzzled about this incident because I have never before considered the possibility that my enemy might be so subject to the Holy Spirit dwelling within me that he would be forced to present himself for direction. After doing some research I can only conclude that this spirit followed my grandson into the house because he was directed to follow him. He did not realize that he had been bound from entering my home. (I constantly pray over my home to keep the adversaries away and on the outside.) When he found himself where he had no business to be his only choice was to show himself to the person with the authority.

3. (New personal account) As a public speaker I travel a lot on business and must stay in many hotels across the country. One night I was tired but went to my room. Unexpectedly, this spirit entered my room and into my dreams. I was being choked and could not breathe. When I came to understand what was happening to me I called on the Lord who sent the spirit on his way and rescued me. This was the first time such a thing had happened to me and I was horrified. I was so afraid that I kept all the lights on all night and had a really hard time sleeping.

4. Another night during my travels after the end of a busy day in Colorado, I stepped off the elevator heading toward my room. I immediately became aware that a very strong evil spirit had fallen into step beside me as I came off the elevator. I had never felt such horror and fear. The fear was over powering and I could feel that this entity

was very strong and tall, reaching to the ceiling. This was the second such attack and I was prepared like I had not been during the first attack. When I reached the door of my room I stopped, placed my hand on the door and said a silent prayer, "Lord, I bind this spirit from entering my room. Protect me in the Name of Jesus". I entered the room and although I was still nervous, the spirit did not enter my room and I was able to sleep through the night.

5. These spiritual attacks continued and began to happen at my home. I have been choked and threatened. Sometimes it happened in my sleep and sometimes I was awake. These attacks became more and more frequent until it was necessary to seek help from other believers. Three of us bound together according to the word of the Lord. We were on the telephone and immediately we could feel the presence of the Lord. We received confirmation that this would not happen again with this spirit. We asked God to cast this spirit into outer darkness. The attacks stopped after two years.

6. Many years ago I was traveling on business in New Orleans. My co-worker with whom I was traveling was determined to look around in one of the stores featuring the occult. I did not want to go into the store, but my co-worker was persistent and so I agreed to enter the store. As I stepped across the threshold I began choking and losing my breath. The stench smelled like burnt sulfur. I could not breathe and left immediately. My co-worker came out and asked what was wrong, and insisted that I come in with her. She noticed nothing out of the ordinary. I went back in the door and the same thing happened. The man working the counter came up to me and I could see the spirit of evil in his eyes as he walked toward me. He said, "You don't belong in here". I left. I now understand how God feels when he is in the presence of sin. It was disgusting, and the Holy Spirit would not remain in such a place. I firmly believe that if I had stayed in that place for much longer the Holy Spirit would have left me. Sometimes we make choices. We are not ever supposed to give place to the devil.

7. This reenactment happened to another person. I was on my knees in my nightly prayer when I felt the presence of a powerful demon come into the room. The fear was emanating from his presence and I knew he wanted to make me afraid. I have faith that the Lord is stronger than the devil and immediately commanded the spirit to leave in the Name of Jesus. The spirit was banished and I went to bed. Unfortunately, he was not gone. For the next two nights he came back with renewed power and energy to frighten me. On the third night I realized that this spirit was very powerful and in my current state of spiritual readiness I could not hope to vanquish him. I was already on my knees so I spoke to the Lord, "This spirit has entered my home for three nights. I have commanded him to leave in the Name of Jesus and he leaves but comes back. Would you please send a warrior angel to get him out of my home and send him into outer darkness"? I got off my knees and got into bed. I could still feel the presence of my enemy as I turned off the light. I felt the angel when he entered my bedroom and the fight began. The most amazing battle took

place round my bed and in the spirit I could actually hear the footsteps and feel the battle that took place because my bed shook. After a time there was no more movement and they were gone. That spirit has never troubled me again.

8. This account comes from another person. He is not presently where he needs to be in God and knows it. My purpose for giving this account is to let you know that anyone is subject to spiritual encounters at any time. You do not have to be a prayed up spirit filled believer for the adversary to come against you. *I was sleeping when* I began dreaming that a very strong evil spirit entered my bedroom. He jerked me out of bed and threw me onto the floor on my knees. He was holding a gun to my head and trying to kill me. He pistol whipped me across the head and threatened to kill me. He put the gun to my head and pulled the trigger. The gun would not fire so he dropped the clip to see if it was loaded and I could see that it *was* loaded. He put the clip back into the gun and again tried to shoot me in the head. The gun would not go off. He was very

angry! About this time my dog was in the house and became disturbed by the presence of the spirit in the house and began barking loudly. My wife awakened and started screaming. She could see the same figure standing menacingly in the doorway that my dog saw. She was finally able to awaken me and the spirit left. I had a hard time getting back to sleep after this experience. We all did.

9. I am acquainted with an unsaved person who has had many encounters with the devil. He has endured endless numbers of spiritual attacks. This person has been attacked when he is awake and in his sleep. If he drinks beer or other hard liquor the attacks are really vicious and he can actually see these demons in the room with him. He has many times called for help from people he know who have the ability to pray and bind these spirits. Several years ago he was visiting out of town. While he was sleeping he felt an evil presence trying to overcome him. He cried out for his mother to help him. Seventy miles away his mother heard his cry and was awakened. She began praying for his protection. When his

mother began praying, the spirit continued for some time to attack, but he could see his mother enter the room and lie across him in a protective posture. God hears our cries and works miracles. His mother prayed constantly for his deliverance. She still believes that God will save him before it is too late.

The reason for recounting these personal attacks is to give an example of how many different ways these attacks may come to you. The devil has no love for you and will use every means at his disposal to bring you down. He has patience and does not give up easily. He comes back again and again and again. It is up to you to get yourself prayed up and covered with the whole armor of God so that you can resist the fiery darts that your adversary brings against you.

Notes

Prayer

Father, I take on myself the whole armor of God. Cover me with protection as I enter the arena of spiritual warfare. Please give me the strength to face my adversary and be victorious, In Jesus Name.

Last Word

The world we live in is not the world of our fathers. Life is fast and can be hard. Technology is changing so rapidly that the software changes before we can pay for the computers and cell phones we already have. Multi-tasking is the name of the game. As Christians it is important to know that we *cannot* multi-task our prayer life, or our relationship with God. Some things require your full attention.

If you are a victim of spiritual attacks, or have spiritual encounters, it is important to find a place in prayer where you can conquer your adversary. At the beginning of this book I stated that when you are born again you receive the power to deal with your enemy.

Having the power, and having the ability to wield that power are two very different sides of the coin. You received the power to take authority over demons when you were filled with the Holy Spirit. Understanding this power and gaining the ability to take authority over demons comes from prayer and fasting. There is no other way to make it happen! In Mark chapter 9 there is a story about the child of a man they met who had been attacked with a deaf and dumb spirit...

> *17And one of the multitude answered and said, Master, I have brought unto thee my son, which hath a dumb spirit;*
>
> *18And wheresoever he taketh him, he teareth him: and he foameth, and gnasheth with his teeth, and pineth away: and I spake to thy disciples that they should cast him out; and they could not.*
>
> *19He answereth him, and saith, O faithless generation, how long shall I be with you? how long shall I suffer you? bring him unto me.*
>
> *20And they brought him unto him: and when he saw him, straightway the spirit tare him; and he fell on the ground, and wallowed foaming.*

21And he asked his father, How long is it ago since this came unto him? And he said, Of a child.

22And ofttimes it hath cast him into the fire, and into the waters, to destroy him: but if thou canst do any thing, have compassion on us, and help us.

23Jesus said unto him, **If thou canst believe, all things are possible to him that believeth.**

24And straightway the father of the child cried out, and said with tears, **Lord, I believe; help thou mine unbelief.**

25When Jesus saw that the people came running together, he rebuked the foul spirit, saying unto him, Thou dumb and deaf spirit, I charge thee, come out of him, and enter no more into him.

26And the spirit cried, and rent him sore, and came out of him: and he was as one dead; insomuch that many said, He is dead.

27But Jesus took him by the hand, and lifted him up; and he arose.

28And when he was come into the house, his disciples asked him privately, Why could not we cast him out?

29And he said unto them, **This kind can come forth by nothing, but by prayer and fasting.** *Mark 9:17-29*

The disciples learned a serious lesson about prayer and fasting. Remember that the Holy Ghost had not been poured out at this time because Jesus still walked the earth so the disciples were still learning how to pray. They were learning what works and does not work. This story is also about **belief**. Jesus called his disciples a faithless generation. In verse 23 he said if you can believe, all things are possible. This is a teaching story about casting out devils, but it is applicable to our situation as well. The *means* you will use to overcome the power of the devil in your life will be through the power of the Holy Ghost with prayer and fasting.

Now, there is a lot of *talk* about prayer. We love to spend time talking about prayer, but I wonder how many of us actually spend time in conversation with God? The truth of the matter is that no amount of talking *about* prayer will get the job done. The only way to gain power with God is to spend time in private and corporate conversation with the Lord. There is no other way for this to happen!

As a people we officially believe in the power of prayer. In private we sometimes do not *do the deed*...We resist taking time to pray because the devil puts up roadblocks to our time schedule that gives us time alone with the Lord. We want to pray and then something happens...A quarrel with the spouse. A disappointment on the job, a pipe breaks under the sink...the list goes on and on. We must put prayer at the top of our list of priorities!

You may think that you do not have a list or do not prioritize your life, but that is erroneous thinking. Even if your life is very simple and you are a stay at home mom or retired person, you set priorities every day of your life. You decide every morning what you will do with the day. Prayer should top the list. The question becomes, *how strongly do I believe that prayer changes things? Do I really believe what I have been professing?* If you truly believe that God can change the course of human events, it is beyond foolish not to make it a priority to have that very important conversation with the Lord every day of your life.

Points to Ponder
1. Prayer is the lifeline of the soul

2. Prayer is the means to defeating the adversary
3. Prayer is a conversation with God
4. Prayer works
5. What are my priorities?
6. How strongly do I believe that prayer works?
7. What are my goals with regard to my relationship to God?
8. Do I *want* to overcome my adversary? Well, do I?
9. Do I believe I *can* overcome my adversary?

You can bind your enemy. You can rebuke your enemy. However, if the demonic attacks are unrelenting and your life is being thrown into chaos, you may be forced to make a head-on attack at the devil. Remember you can ask for angelic protection. You can ask for strength and confidence to face your adversary. When you do this kind of praying, make certain you have been in prayer and fasting. Be explicit. Say exactly what you mean. You can take authority over the enemy. The angels of God will protect you. You can have peace.

When you enter the arena of spiritual warfare you will have surprises... Your prayers will become longer. You will delight in your conversations with the Lord. You will be stronger. You will find a new depth in your walk with the Lord.

Prayer

Satan, I take authority over you In the Name of Jesus Christ. This home belongs to God. We (name everyone living in the home) do not belong to you. Remove your demons and familiar spirits from my home. None of you are to enter my property or my home again. In the name of Jesus Christ.

This is a bold prayer. However, desperate times require desperate, determined efforts. The Holy Spirit within you gives you the authority to forbid these spirits entry to your home. You must be prayerful and in touch with the Lord, but you have the Power. *Remember Acts: 2:8 But you will receive power when the Holy Spirit comes on you...*

God loves you and wants you to live an overcoming life. He gave us the plan of salvation in simple terms so that we may lay hold on eternal life. Purpose in your heart that *nothing* in this world will come between you and your God. The devil desires your soul but he cannot have it if you choose God. The choice is yours. Learn to fight your enemy and be an over comer. Choose eternal life!

Notes

Made in the USA